Boston Harbor Islands
National Park Area

Dedication

With remarkable foresight, a quarter of a century before the United States Congress acted, State Senator Joe Moakley succeeded in conferring upon the Boston Harbor Islands the protective status of a Massachusetts State Park.

In doing so, and in the nick of time, he set the stage for all that was—and is—to come in this uniquely magnificent harbor setting.

Senator Joe Moakley

If authoring the federal legislation to designate these islands as a unit of the national park system makes me the father of the effort to preserve these treasures for future generations, then surely Congressman Moakley is its grandfather.

Although he had much to be proud of in a long and extraordinarily productive career, he often told me that his early intervention on behalf of the Boston Harbor Islands was among his proudest achievements. Now, as this wonderful scenery becomes increasingly accessible and enjoyable, it is fitting that we remember who set the stage.

Gerry E. Studds, Former United States Congressman 10th District, Commonwealth of Massachusetts

Boston Harbor Islands
National Park Area

The West Head of Peddocks Island and its small marsh are visible at the middle, left of this bird's-eye view of the island. Spectacle, Long, Rainsford, Gallops, Lovells, and Georges Islands appear on the horizon from left to right.

ISBN 0892725915

Designed by Chilton Creative
All photographs by Ken Mallory unless otherwise noted

5   4   3   2   1

Printed in China

Down East Books
P.O. Box 679
Camden, ME 04843
BOOK ORDERS: telephone 1-800-685-7962 or visit
www.downeastbooks.com

Library of Congress Control Number: 2003102656

Table of Contents

A Hingham Harbor sunset (photo, above) is the setting for the host of recreational boats that explore Boston Harbor during the summer. The South Shore is only one of several entryways to the Boston Harbor Islands national park area.

These great egret chicks perched in a giant nest above ground (photo, left) are examples of birds that use the harbor to nest and forage for food.

Acknowledgments

The Boston Harbor Islands national park area's roots go back to proposals in the late 1800s by landscape architects Frederick Law Olmsted Sr. and Charles Eliot to expand maritime recreation. The Metropolitan Park Commission's 1890s vision to incorporate the islands into the Metropolitan Park System was realized when the Boston Harbor Islands State Park was created in the 1970s. The stewardship continues as a part of the new national park area.

The authors and photographers would like to acknowledge the support and contributions of many partners in creating this book, which would not have been possible without their help. Thanks are due to Kathy Abbott and the Island Alliance for securing financial support from Massachusetts Environmental Trust and for helping guide the book's content and approach; to George Price, Sarah Peskin, Barbara Mackey, and Bruce Jacobson of the National Park Service for contributing content and providing encouragement and support; to Modern Continental for funding administrative support; and to all the partners that have helped create the Boston Harbor Islands National Park Area and that are committed to sustaining it in the future. The Partners include National Park Service, United States Coast Guard, Massachusetts Department of Environmental Management, Metropolitan District Commission, Massachusetts Port Authority, Massachusetts Water Resources Authority, City of Boston, Boston Redevelopment Authority, Thompson Island Outward Bound Education Center, The Trustees of Reservations, Island Alliance, and the Boston Harbor Islands Advisory Council.

Special thanks as well to Margaret Thompson of Wellesley College for her help with the geology section of the book; Christine Arato of the National Park Service; Shapins Associates Inc. for the individual island maps; and the overview map of all the islands; Dale Levering, author of *An Illustrated Flora of the Boston Harbor Islands*; and Margaret Thompson Mallory for many of the best photos used in this book. Larry Lowenthal deserves credit as the primary writer of the book's text, especially the individual island descriptions, Moses Sweetser, author of *King's Handbook of Boston Harbor*, originally published in 1882 and reprinted by Friends of Boston Harbor Islands, should be credited as one of the first individuals to perceive the harbor and its islands as a cohesive entity and to draw attention to its value.

Finally, we would like to express thanks to the New England Aquarium; to Jerry R. Schubel, president emeritus of the New England Aquarium; Brian MacDonald, aquarium director of sales; Sukey Padewar, aquarium education department senior program developer; Jen Goebel, former senior publicist/publications coordinator; and aquarium volunteer David Perrin for helping to make this book possible.

The island information kiosk next to Long Wharf is the island visitor's introduction to the over thirty islands in the Boston Harbor Islands national park area. Next page: With the icon of Boston Light on a welcoming flag, island goers get ready to board one of the park ferries at Long Wharf, just opposite the New England Aquarium.

What Is the Boston Harbors Islands National Park Area?

The Boston Harbor Islands became a unit of the national park system in November 1996 by an act of Congress that contains several provisions which, in total, make this a national park like no other. It includes thirty islands that lie within the large "C" shape of Boston Harbor. Managed by a unique partnership, the islands have been closely linked to Massachusetts Bay and to coastal communities for thousands of years (see box for a list of the Boston Harbor Islands partnership members).

The land mass of the Boston Harbor Islands national park area totals approximately 1,600 acres. It extends seaward eleven miles from downtown Boston. The Boston Harbor

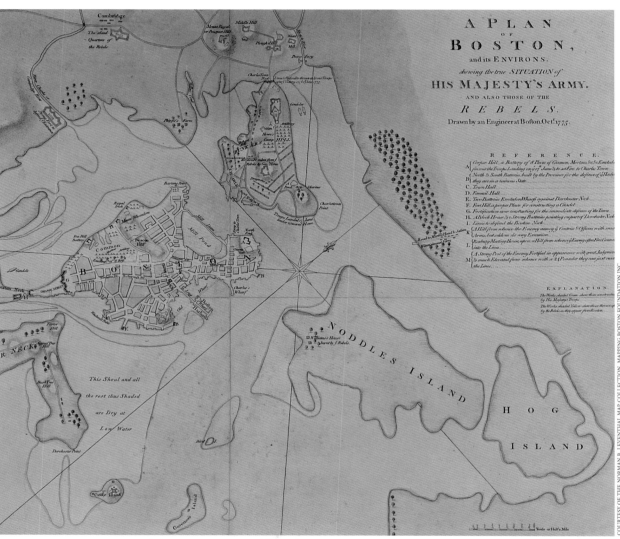

Boston and its harbor looked a lot different during the early European settlement years in the 1600s (map, above). Boston has achieved its distinctive shape today by filling in the tidal flats surrounding its peninsula. Graves Lighthouse (photo, left) is an unmanned, granite tower operated by the United States Coast Guard. At 113 feet, it is the tallest lighthouse in Boston Harbor. It was built in 1905, and today its light and horn are powered by solar panels.

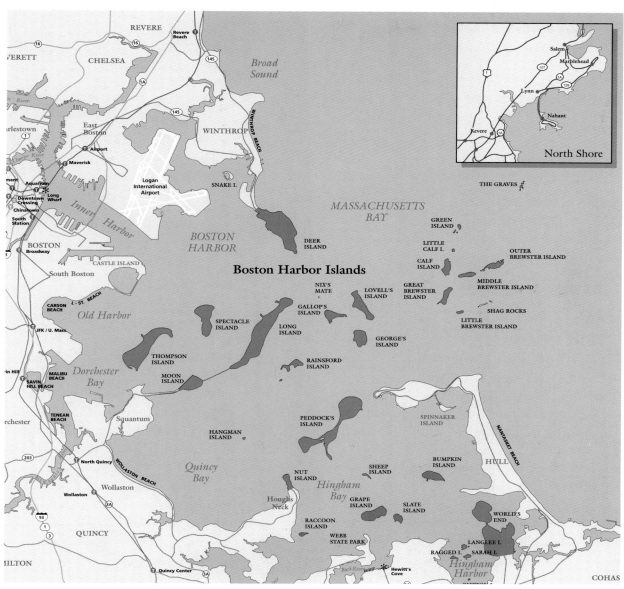

REVERE

Revere Beach

CHELSEA

EVERETT

16

16

145

1A

Broad Sound

East Boston

Airport

Maverick

WINTHROP

145

WINTHROP BEACH

Logan International Airport

SNAKE I.

North Shore

Salem

Marblehead

1

107

1A

Lynn

129

Nahant

Revere

1A

MASSACHUSETTS BAY

THE GRAVES

Aquarium

Long Wharf

Downtown Crossing

Chinatown

South Station

Inner Harbor

BOSTON HARBOR

DEER ISLAND

GREEN ISLAND

LITTLE CALF I.

CALF ISLAND

OUTER BREWSTER ISLAND

BOSTON

Broadway

CASTLE ISLAND

South Boston

BOSTON HARBOR ISLANDS

Boston Harbor Islands

NIX'S MATE

LOVELL'S ISLAND

GREAT BREWSTER ISLAND

MIDDLE BREWSTER ISLAND

CARSON BEACH

Old Harbor

L ST. BEACH

GALLOP'S ISLAND

SHAG ROCKS

JFK / U. Mass.

SPECTACLE ISLAND

LONG ISLAND

LITTLE BREWSTER ISLAND

THOMPSON ISLAND

GEORGE'S ISLAND

Dorchester Bay

MALIBU BEACH

MOON ISLAND

RAINSFORD ISLAND

SAVIN HILL BEACH

203

orchester

TENEAN BEACH

Squantum

HANGMAN ISLAND

PEDDOCK'S ISLAND

SPINNAKER ISLAND

NANTASKET BEACH

North Quincy

WOLLASTON BEACH

HULL

Quincy Bay

NUT ISLAND

SHEEP ISLAND

BUMPKIN ISLAND

Wollaston

Wollaston

3A

Houghs Neck

Hingham Bay

GRAPE ISLAND

SLATE ISLAND

WORLD'S END

93

1

3

QUINCY

RACCOON ISLAND

WEBB STATE PARK

LANGLEE I.

RAGGED I.   SARAH I.

ILTON

Quincy Center

3A

Back River

Hewitt's Cove

Hingham Harbor

COHAS

The Boston Harbor Islands national park area islands are colored brown in the map above. Beachcombing and tidepool exploring are some of the favorite activities for park visitors shown here on Lovells Island (photo, right).

Islands form a transition between the open ocean and the settled coast, between the world beyond Boston Harbor and the features specific to it. They are not only a physical entrance but also a gateway to a long span of history, from Native American uses through the explosive growth of the city and industry and the concerns of the current postindustrial age. Thirty-five miles of relatively undeveloped shoreline within a densely settled urban area, resources associated with thousands of years of occupation by American Indians, and the complex natural communities of the intertidal zones all illustrate the intrinsic value of Boston Harbor Islands resources.

Both literally and symbolically, the islands offer a unique vantage point from which visitors can contemplate metropolitan growth and change. The islands also offer an exceptional perspective on change in the region's ecosystem. Magnificent open spaces surrounded by expanses of water, the islands vividly illustrate the region's complex geological past and the continual effect of natural processes on their habitats, their uses, and even their shapes. From them, visitors can learn about how such complex ecosystems as harbors are revived. The improvement in the cleanliness of Boston Harbor waters has regenerated the biological communities of the islands and the sea around them, and has made possible an impressively wide range of recreational uses. Thus the islands are both a haven for urban residents and tourists and a

The harbor islands offer breathtaking views of Boston including sunsets like the one above.

highly effective laboratory in which to learn about natural change, cultural history, and stewardship.

Until 1970, when the Commonwealth of Massachusetts began systematically to acquire them for the benefit of the public, the islands of Boston Harbor had been shielded from public view and appreciation for generations. The culprits were commercial and industrial development along the waterfront and the poor quality of harbor water. In 1985, Boston Harbor was labeled the most polluted in the nation, but the dramatic recovery of water quality during the 1990s, through the Massachusetts Water Resources Authority's wastewater treatment plan, contributed to widespread support for establishing a national park area. Now, after an investment of more than $4 billion in better wastewater manage-

ment, the harbor is cleaner and more inviting. Over the past three decades, numerous public and private agencies have once again turned their focus to Boston Harbor and its islands, as the region seeks to rebuild its historical and ecological ties to Massachusetts Bay.

The more than thirty islands of Boston Harbor, ranging in size from less than 1 acre to 274 acres, have served numerous public and private uses, and are a unique example of an island cluster intimately tied to the life of a city. Although within sight of a dynamic and densely populated metropolitan area, they continue to offer the visitor a rare sense of isolation. Their proximity to a large urban population and their special natural, geological, cultural, and historic resources, and the values associated with them, contribute to their national significance.

Four of the five drumlins that make up Peddocks Island reach out toward the peninsula of Hull in the background (photo, left).

Staghorn sumac (photo, above) display clusters of flowers in the spring, then develop into maroon colored fruits in July and mid-summer. Staghorn sumac fruits produce a refreshing lemonade-like drink. Its upper stems and flower stalks are velvety, like newly forming stag antlers, thus the name. Male and female flowers occur on different plants.

Journey to the Islands

With New England Aquarium at the center of this photo of Boston, one of the harbor islands' most important gateways, Long Wharf (bottom right in photo) welcomes island visitors for their journey to Georges and other island attractions. The Custom House stands spire-like behind the Aquarium, and Long Wharf sits in front of the Marriott Hotel, the brick structure that resembles an ocean liner with a rounded prow.

Just beyond the shadows of the skyscrapers that dominate downtown Boston's waterfront lies the Boston Harbor Islands National Park Area. With more than thirty islands, it offers a variety of recreational opportunities, scenic landscapes, wilderness, and historic landmarks that tell stories of the region's rich and colorful past.

Passenger ferries leave regularly from several mainland locations for the Boston Harbor Islands. Boston and Hingham are the most popular departure points. For this journey, we'll take the downtown Boston to Georges Island ferry, which has served the islands since the 1960s. The boat leaves from Long Wharf, one of three National Historic Landmarks in the park.

As our ferry pulls away from Long Wharf, the oldest continuously operating wharf in the country, we are reminded of Boston's economic connection between land and sea. Long Wharf, extended several times to its present 1,586 feet, was the city's link to the sea, and the captains of commerce never wanted to lose this grip.

It was not always that way. The Puritans who established the Massachusetts Bay Colony hoped to create a commonwealth of independent small farmers, and much of Massachusetts retained that character into the 19th-century. But on the coast, maritime opportunities were too tempting—and too profitable—to ignore. It wasn't long before Boston became the leading trade port in the original thirteen colonies.

Though no longer Boston's tallest building, nor even its center of maritime commerce, the Custom House and its distinctive clock tower serve as a reminder of the city's maritime past. Within this view, we are treated to a number of other more modern sites—Rowe's Wharf, the John Joseph Moakley United States Courthouse (home of the park's Discovery Center)—as well as attractions such as the New England Aquarium and some of Boston's well-known waterfront restaurants.

As we make our way through the inner harbor, the Leonard Zakim Bunker Hill Bridge to the northwest helps to orient us. In clear weather the masts of the U.S.S. *Constitution*

The journey to Georges Island promises spectacular views of the city and a sense that ferryboat travelers are beginning a new adventure.

("Old Ironsides") in Charlestown Navy Yard can be seen. Two famous landmarks of the Freedom Trail—North Church in Boston, and the Bunker Hill Monument in Charlestown—are plainly visible as well.

To our right as we head east, the point of land known as Castle Island marks the end of Boston's Inner Harbor just after the bustling Black Falcon Cruise Terminal. Although now connected to the mainland (it was at one time an island), Castle Island's strategic location played a significant role in the long history of

BOSTON HARBOR ISLANDS PARTNERSHIP
408 Atlantic Avenue, Suite 228
Boston MA 02110-3350
Telephone: 617-223-8666
BostonIslands.com

Information Kiosk: Located at Long Wharf, Boston. Rangers and volunteers provide public information and orientation to the Boston Harbor Islands.

NATIONAL PARK AREA DISCOVERY CENTER

Located at John Joseph Moakley United States Courthouse, Fan Pier, South Boston waterfront, where interactive video offers a virtual tour of Boston Light and Little Brewster Island, Grape Island, and Georges Islands, as well as a soaring trip "as the gull flies" over all thirty islands in the park. Also staffed information desk in season; books and other island-related sales items; and restrooms.

TRAVEL BASICS

Operating Hours, Seasons: During the summer season, the islands are open daily from 9:00 A.M. until sunset. During the spring and fall the islands are open on weekends. Special arrangements for school groups are possible for weekdays in spring, summer, and fall seasons. Some sites have additional hours.

GETTING TO THE ISLANDS

Public Transportation: Passenger ferries link the islands to the mainland at several locations. Access is from downtown Boston and also from Hingham, Hull, and Quincy on the South Shore. In season, regularly scheduled ferries connect to Georges Island where water

shuttles take visitors to other islands. Private boats may rent moorings or anchor offshore. The Massachusetts Bay Transit Authority connects to the major departure points for the islands.

ACCESSIBILITY

The islands are not fully accessible for disabled visitors. Ferry vessels are accessible by wheelchair with staff assistance, but getting off the boat onto the islands may be difficult because of the ramps. Spectacle, Georges, and Peddocks are most accessible for wheelchair use.

CAMPING

Four islands offer primitive camping within sight of downtown Boston. The camping season starts in May and continues through Columbus Day weekend in October. Permits and reservations are required. Access is by boat only. No pets are allowed on the Boston Harbor Islands. For help in deciding which island meets your camping needs call 617-223-8666.

WEATHER & CLIMATE

Weather is variable, from clear, crisp days to stormy, chilly days. Water breezes make for cooler ferry rides, requiring jackets or windbreakers. Walking shoes, hats, drinking water, and sunscreen are essential. Binoculars are highly recommended.

The inner harbor boat journey to Georges Island begins at the city skyline (upper middle in photo) continues past Massport's Conley Terminal for containerized shipments (middle of photo with red and blue containers), until it passes Castle Island and Fort Independence (photo, foreground).

An airplane taxies along one of Logan International Airport's runways that border the inner harbor waterway.

Once a 12-acre island, Nixes Mate is today reduced to a channel marker protected by a wall of rock and cement.

defending the port of Boston. Today the point is dominated by Fort Independence, a mammoth, five-bastioned, granite-walled fortress. The current granite fort was built between the years 1834 and 1851. Castle Island itself is the oldest continually fortified site on British North America. Fort Independence was decommissioned following World War II.

A monument visible on the shore of Castle Island honors Donald McKay, builder of the clipper ship *Flying Cloud* which, in 1851, sailed from New York to San Francisco in a record eighty-nine days. McKay's shipyard was actually located on the opposite side of the harbor, on an island that has since been incorporated into the East Boston waterfront. Gone too are three adjacent islands: Governors, Apple, and Bird. All were leveled and connected to form the runways at Logan International

Airport, now a transportation hub where 26 million passengers are served annually.

Beyond Castle Island we enter President Roads (known as King's Road prior to the American Revolution). This is Boston Harbor's main shipping channel. Here, as the city skyline recedes, we find ourselves at the "entrance" to the Boston Harbor Islands National Park Area. On our right, is dome-shaped Spectacle Island. At one time the most abused of the harbor islands—having hosted a horse-rendering plant and city dump—Spectacle now epitomizes the harbor's renewal. Once shunned, the island has become a hub, with a new visitor center, beaches, and trails.

Next on our right is Long Island, the largest of Boston's harbor islands. Its rugged northern head stands out, accentuated by a lighthouse. This light, which is no longer manned, dates to 1819. It provides our first

encounter with one of the defining elements of the harbor islands: aids to navigation.

The two enfolding arms of Long and Deer Islands seem to embrace and shelter the inner harbor. Although once separate, Deer Island is today an extension of the Winthrop peninsula, visible on our left just beyond Logan Airport.

Among the most powerful symbols of Boston Harbor's renaissance are the egg-shaped sludge digesters on Deer Island. They are an integral part of the process of recycling sewage sludge into fertilizer and represent a massive public commitment to clean up a harbor that was one of the filthiest in the United States. The return of harbor porpoises, the improved health of edible fish, and cleaner, more inviting beaches are testament to the harbor's rebirth.

An odd black-and-white pyramid marks the location of nearby Nixes Mate, part of the Boston Harbor Islands park. In colonial times, this island covered 12 acres. Erosion caused by constantly pounding surf, and probably by quarrying, has reduced its size to a spit of sand visible at low tide. Nixes Mate contributed in a bizarre way to maritime safety in the 1700s, when the body of a pirate who had been hanged for his offenses was displayed there as a warning to others who might have been tempted to follow the black flag.

As we approach Georges Island, Gallops, and Lovells Islands lie to our left. These three mid-size islands are rich in history and inviting for modern recreational use. All experienced important military episodes. Gallops—though smaller—was the site of a major public-health facility.

Gallops is comprised of what is known in geological parlance as a drumlin, while Lovells is formed by three connected drumlins. Drumlins were formed when continental glaciers slid over and smoothed earlier glacial deposits. In the Boston region not all drumlins are oriented in the same direction, as one would expect if they had been produced in a single glacial episode. We know that during the Pleistocene epoch, which began about 2.5 million years ago, ice sheets advanced deep into Europe and North America at least four different times.

Georges Island is one of the jewels of the harbor island group. Fort Warren, which covers most of the island, is the outstanding historic structure on the harbor islands, the crowning example of their history of military use and one of the three national historic landmarks. Georges Island's easy accessibility allows you to explore the fort's ramparts and parade grounds, picnic at the water's edge, set fishing lines in the bay, and then catch a boat back into the city.

For many visitors, Georges Island may be the only stop in their exploration of the Boston Harbor Islands. But if you can, let Georges and other key locations in the continuing development of the park, such as Spectacle and Peddocks Islands, be bases for

With its rich maritime history and miles of shoreline, Boston Harbor has shown itself to be an ideal location for events like the Tall Ships parade.

further exploration. They are windows on a world of other harbor islands, each with its own history, personality, and activities. There are children's festivals and treasure quests, overnight camping, nature walks, concerts, ocean-rowing contests, sea kayaking, and wildlife tours that offer a chance to glimpse oyster catchers, many kinds of sea ducks, sea birds, and harbor seals. In the fall, you can celebrate Halloween harbor-island style, enjoy apple picking and attend Native American festivals. At the end of the year there are cruises to observe birds and marine mammals in winter.

For the historians among you, explore the early history of the islands with park rangers. The islands are the sentinels of Boston Harbor, used by Native Americans for thousands of years and, more recently, evidence of more than two hundred buildings and structures, sea walls, forts, lighthouses, gun emplacements, concrete bunkers, and brick military buildings. Much of their history is on display for you to explore, and as military historian Bill Stokinger has observed, "All of the islands are special. You have to talk to them, and then you have to listen to what they have to say."

The Islands

Boston Light is one of the crown jewels of the Boston Harbor Islands, a welcome beacon for mariners as they approach Boston and the other harbor islands shown here: Georges and Rainsford (in photo, upper left), and Lovells and Gallops (right), with Long Island and its checkerboard water tower in the distance (middle, right).

Bumpkin Island

The trailing spit of Bumpkin's sandbar (in photo, bottom edge) leads out toward Hull peninsula to the south looking like a spar at the stem of a ship, while the island's welcoming dock (near the top of Bumpkin) faces Slate and Grape Islands and Webb State Park near the entrance to the Back River in Weymouth.

At low tide, when Bumpkin Island is nearly connected to the Hull Peninsula, it is easy to understand how the peninsula itself was formed by ocean currents piling up sandbars to link separate drumlins. We are always reminded that the Harbor Islands are poised on the edge of geological change and that, unlike the situation at many national parks, the work of these forces are visible.

Bumpkin Island is a single, symmetrical drumlin falling away to a rock-strewn shoreline. Its seventy-foot height affords views toward the southeastern reaches of the Harbor Islands park area and the town of Hull. A shelter on the island's northwest side provides views of Boston, Peddocks Island, and Worlds End.

Throughout its history, Bumpkin Island has had various names including Round, Bomkin, Ward's, and Pumpkin. Its current moniker likely derives from the island's shape, specifically its prominent eastern spit. In nautical parlance, a bumpkin is a projecting boom or a spar at the stern of a ship.

The island has supported many traditional harbor island uses. Close to the mainland, elevated, and featuring a variety of resources, it was frequented by Native Americans. In 1681 Samuel Ward, who had purchased the island from the town of Weymouth, bequeathed it to Harvard College to provide a source of income from tenant farmers.

Beginning in 1900, Boston philanthropist Albert C. Burrage leased the island from Harvard and established a hospital for children with physical disabilities. Patients spent summers here free of charge. A foundation with thousands of yellow bricks is all that remains of the hospital after it was destroyed by fire in 1945. During World War I, Burrage gave permission to the federal government to construct a naval training station on the island. Most of this facility, which once contained fifty-six buildings and graduated nearly fifteen thousand seamen, was dismantled after the war, but traces remain.

Generally the varied uses of Bumpkin have been benign and have not left the scars evident on other islands. A long-abandoned cobblestone farmhouse is one of the more conspicuous man-made features still extant. Vines and small trees soften what remains of the naval training station.

This stone house dates from the 1800s (photo, left). It was used originally as a home and then as a heating plant for the former Children's hospital and for the Naval Training Station. Blueberries are plentiful on this and many other islands (photo, below).

Bumpkin at a Glance

Access: Ferry from Hingham or free inter-island water shuttle via Georges Island.

Description: At 35 acres, this is one of the smaller Boston Harbor Islands. There are rocky beaches, tidal flats, wooded areas, open fields, and marked trails.

Facilities: Self-guided trail map available. Composting toilets, picnic areas, hiking trails, benches, and shade shelters provided. Seasonal rangers, tours, and special events. Individual and group camping allowed. No running water or electricity.

Special Interest: There are remains of military and farm buildings and walkways of a former hospital for disabled children. This is a good site for group camping and habitat exploration.

Agency: Massachusetts Department of Environmental Management

Staghorn sumac trees (photo, above) frame the remains of a once flourishing Naval Training Station mess hall. Beginning around World War I, the United States Navy covered the island with temporary wooden buildings to support the training facility.

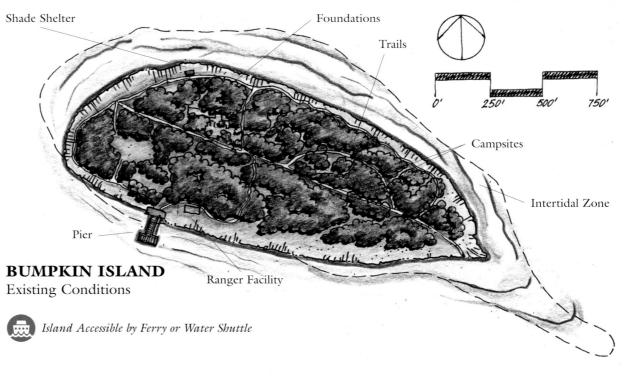

BUMPKIN ISLAND
Existing Conditions

Island Accessible by Ferry or Water Shuttle

Deer Island

Certain islands exemplify activities that were once common on many of Boston's harbor islands. On Georges Island military matters are inescapable. Maritime safety is clearly the dominant theme on Little Brewster. On Deer Island the mundane but critical subject of sewage treatment is front and center.

Sewage treatment is one of those subjects most city planners don't like to think about, yet it is essential. Historically cities ignored the problem as long as possible. When finally forced to deal with it, the first solution was to send the offending material "away." As an edge environment, Boston Harbor was an obvious choice for sewage disposal. It was the same philosophy that located numerous institutions on the harbor islands: they were necessary, but the public preferred to keep them out of sight.

In time, pollution too overwhelming to ignore taught us that there is no "away." Today Deer Island's wastewater treatment plant reflects a more responsible attitude. Protecting against the daily onslaught of sewage that had once contaminated Boston Harbor waters and fouled beaches, the facility helps visitors enjoy the restored richness and beauty of the harbor and its islands.

The treatment plant is managed by the Massachusetts Water Resources Authority (MWRA). Two-thirds of the island's 210 acres are taken up by the treatment plant, with 60 acres of surrounding open space. The new treatment plant, with a peak capacity of 1.27

In this aerial view of Deer Island the egg-shaped sludge digesters are the most easily identifiable component of the 110-acre, 1.2-billion-gallon-per-day Deer Island Wastewater Treatment Plant that now protects Boston Harbor. The walkways and man-made hills on the island's perimeter offer views into the treatment process and out to the city skyline, the harbor's main shipping channel, and islands such as Long, Spectacle, and Gallops. The island has been connected to the mainland since 1938, when hurricane Edna filled the channel separating it from the town of Winthrop.

billion gallons of wastewater per day, cleans the sewage waste stream from forty-three communities with a combined population of 2.5 million people. The plant's twelve 140-foot tall sludge digesters, which resemble giant eggs, form a new landmark in the harbor.

Residents of the Boston metropolitan area have reason to be proud of Deer Island as a symbol of the city's commitment to natural resource protection and environmental stewardship. This success, however, cannot ignore darker chapters of the island's past. Possibly the most shameful episode occurred during King Philip's War in the late 1670s. During the harsh winter of 1675–76, hundreds of

One landmark along Deer Island's 2-mile perimeter path is the historic 1898 Steam Pumping Station. From 1898 until 1968 this station burned coal and wastewater debris to pump raw sewage into Boston Harbor. The renovated station provides visitor orientation and appointment-only meeting space.

Native Americans were held by the colonial government on Deer Island and three other islands. Most of these people were not even part of the native resistance to European settlement, but were friendly toward the English and, in some cases, had even adopted their religion. Left without adequate food, clothing and shelter, many of the captives died. Native Americans return to Deer Island every year in October to commemorate their ancestors' suffering.

Another sorrowful episode unfolded in the 1840s when the Great Famine drove a million or more Irish people to emigrate to the United States. For thousands of them Deer Island was a gateway to a new life, but for hundreds of others it was a graveyard. Many of the refugees were in poor health when they departed and were further weakened by the stressful journey across the ocean. In 1847 the City of Boston established a hospital on Deer Island, which treated nearly 5,000 people between 1847 and 1849. Most recovered, but 750 died and were buried in the island's cemetery.

The island has since been the site of an almshouse, a reformatory, and, most notably, a prison, which in the early 20th-century was the largest prison complex in the state. These were practical uses at the time because Deer Island was separate from the mainland. The great New England hurricane of 1938, however, closed Shirley Gut, a strait that had formerly been navigable for small craft, and ended Deer Island's insular status.

DEER ISLAND
Existing Conditions

Island Accessible by Ferry or Water Shuttle

Gallops Island

During World War II, Gallops Island housed a maritime radio school, with 325 students at a time, as well as a school for bakers and cooks, with another 150 trainees. These men were accommodated in a complex of temporary barracks and other buildings, including a three-story recreation hall. Somehow all this activity was crowded onto one of the smaller (16-acre) islands.

Earlier wars witnessed similar military activity. French troops dug earthworks and mounted cannon here to protect their fleet in Boston Harbor after France became America's ally during the Revolution. During the Civil War, twenty wooden barracks, capable of quartering 3,000 troops, were erected. Here Massachusetts soldiers received basic training and developed regimental cohesion before going south to fight. At the end of the war the famed 54th Massachusetts Regiment of African American volunteers—celebrated in the movie *Glory* and the bronze relief statue in the Boston Common—was mustered out on this island.

Following the Civil War former military buildings were reused as a quarantine hospital. Doctors at this facility examined immigrants, performing the same duties as the better-known stations at Castle Garden and Ellis Island in New York. By 1886 the Gallops Island medical staff was examining over 33,000 passengers a year. In 1916 the U.S. Public Health Service assumed control of the hospital and immigration station.

Gallops Island rises from the shoreline at the bottom of this picture to a vista-filled high ground. Long Island, Spectacle, and Thompson lead the way toward South Boston and the Kennedy Library in the far background.

Because it was not permanently inhabited, Gallops, like other harbor islands, passed through cycles of intense activity, followed by near-abandonment. Today rabbits hop among the foundations of former hospitals and schools. A cemetery on the north end of the island, which holds the graves of people who died at the quarantine hospital, is a dim reminder of former uses.

It is the island's vegetation, rather than bricks and mortar, that recalls earlier activity. From 1927 to 1935 Dr. Alvin Sweeney served as director of the Public Health Service hospital. In his spare time the doctor, a skilled horticulturist, planted trees and ornamental shrubs near the residential campus at the center of the island for the enjoyment of hospital staff. Among the plantings that remain today are spirea (roses), lilac, privet, apple, and peach trees. Probably without realizing it, Dr. Sweeney was repeating an early episode of island history. The first governor of Massachusetts Bay, John Winthrop, planted the first apple and pear trees in New England on Governors Island, now part of Logan Airport. Around the same time, John Gallop was enjoying the "snug farm" on his island.

With the departure of more intensive use, Gallops Island has returned to an earlier role: recreation. In 1833 Margaret Newcomb, the widow of a man who had farmed the island, opened a restaurant and inn that hosted visitors until the onset of the Civil War. That was quite an early date for recreational use,

especially in Boston, where lingering Puritan attitudes looked with suspicion on the idea of enjoyment for its own sake.

The island's seventy-nine-foot summit provides extensive views in all directions. It is a fine observation point from which to see the configuration of this part of the harbor complex, with the old natural channel, The Narrows, to the east and the dredged channel, President's Roads, to the north.

Gallops at a Glance

Access: Gallops Island is currently closed for public visitation following the discovery of asbestos-containing tiles, called transite, on the island. The military used transite in the construction of facilities on the island prior to and during World War II. In the 1950s, the facilities were demolished and debris was buried on the island. Fifty years later, the cover on the debris is eroding and exposing the asbestos tiles. The island will remain closed to visitors while a remediation plan is developed and implemented.

Agency: Massachusetts Department of Environmental Management

GALLOPS ISLAND
Existing Conditions

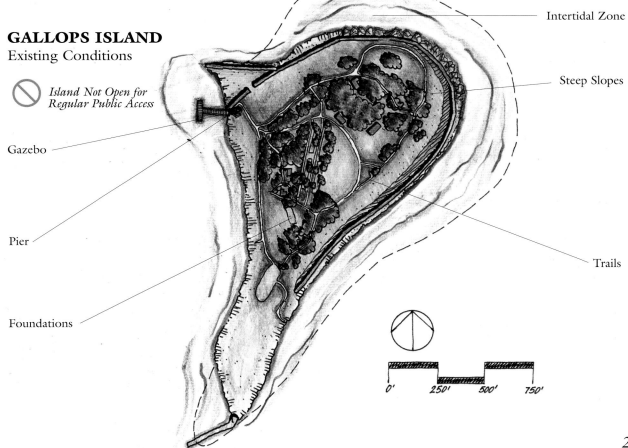

Island Not Open for
Regular Public Access

Gazebo

Pier

Foundations

Intertidal Zone

Steep Slopes

Trails

0' 250' 500' 750'

Georges Island

Georges Island lies at the center of the island cluster that includes Lovells, Gallops, and Peddocks, and this central location determined the island's history. Here the military presence, evident on many of the islands, is inescapable. Fort Warren dominates the scene.

In fact, Georges Island is now so closely identified with Fort Warren that it is difficult to imagine it without this formidable landmark. Early accounts tell us that the island, formed from two drumlins, rose to a similar height as its neighbors. One might assume it was named for a British king, but it lacks royal pretensions and instead carries on the memory of Captain John George, an 18th-century Boston merchant.

There was a brief military introduction during the War for Independence, when the French built earthworks to protect their fleet in Boston Harbor. The island's period of military glory began, however, in 1834, when work started on Fort Warren. Named for patriot hero Joseph Warren, who was killed at the battle of Bunker Hill, the fort was destined to become the keystone of Boston's harbor defenses.

Fort Warren remains a magnificent example of the "Third System" of coastal defense. Sometimes called the "permanent" system, these forts were thought to be the final word in protecting the country's coastal cities and as such were built for the ages. They were situated at a safe distance from the harbor they protected and were intended to concentrate such overwhelming firepower—300 guns in the case of Fort Warren—that no enemy fleet could batter its way past.

The construction of Fort Warren reflects this idea of permanence. Each block of granite was cut and faced by hand to fit its location—a task that took up to two days. The granite came from Quincy—as did the man who supervised the construction—Lt. Col. Sylvanus Thayer, also known as "The Father of West Point." Engineers like Thayer, aware that they were building an enduring edifice, considered pleasing proportions, as

Georges Island is a dominant presence in the harbor islands and one of the most popular destinations. Here it is seen with Lovells Island in the background.

Georges Island served as a prisoner of war camp and training area during the Civil War. An annual summer event celebrates that history with characters dressed to play the part.

well as function, in their design.

The graceful aspects of Fort Warren partially conceal its immense size—nearly a mile around the perimeter. The formidable structure includes ten-foot thick walls, endless labyrinths of prisons and officers' quarters, a sprawling interior parade ground, and massive parapets.

While the fort is impressive for its sheer size, visitors can relate readily to its small-scale features and the human stories they suggest. The bakery makes one think of the monotonous

GEORGES ISLAND
Existing Conditions

 Island Accessible by Ferry or Water Shuttle

Fort Warren

Intertidal Zone

Overlook Building

Ranger Station Maintenance and Snack Bar

Gun Emplacements

Parade Ground

Powder House

Sea Wall

Pier

Shade Shelters

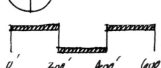

0'   200'   400'   600'

25

daily lives of the soldiers. Even if one is skeptical of the numerous ghost and escape tales, like island storyteller Edward Rowe Snow's beloved *Lady in Black,* it is easy to appreciate how they arose. The impression is heightened when units of re-enactors, both Federal and Confederate, populate the fort.

The presence of Confederates brings up the fact that Fort Warren never faced a foreign foe. Its most notable events took place during the Civil War. Confederate prisoners were held at the fort, among them James Mason and John Slidell, emissaries to Great Britain. Their seizure aboard a British ship almost fulfilled the Confederate government's desire to bring Britain into the war against the United States. After the war, Confederate vice president Alexander Stephens was imprisoned on the island.

Since Fort Warren's builders believed they had achieved permanence and perfection, it must have come as a staggering shock to discover that the fort on which they had lavished such expense and painstaking workmanship was obsolete almost as soon as it was finished. By the end of the Civil War such forts were as outdated as the wooden warships they were built to resist.

Today visitors can appreciate Fort Warren in a more relaxed way. Once intended to command the approach to the harbor, the fort now commands a spectacular view.

For many years Georges Island has been the most visited of the harbor islands, and

Recreational fishermen use Georges to fish for stripers, blues, flounder, and other fishes of the harbor islands.

deservedly so. Whether savoring the view from the high parapets, fishing from the beach, watching seals on the offshore rocks, or picnicking on the perimeter of the fort, visitors seldom regret taking the boat to Georges Island.

Besides the guided tours you can take inside Fort Warren, exhibits like the one shown here (photo above, left) allow visitors to learn about the fort's history on their own. Fort Warren preserves large wells like this one that once contained 12-inch guns that "disappeared"(recoiled) after firing to protect the gun and gun crew. They were built around the beginning of the 20th-century (photo, left). The fort also includes what is called Bastion C with a large parade ground, storehouse areas, barracks, and a large storage magazine for gunpowder (photo, above).

Grape Island

Grape Island is flanked by Slate Island in the photo above. (Slate is at the bottom of the picture.) The view looks back toward Webb Memorial State Park (above left in photo), the entrance to Fore River in Weymouth, and Houghs Neck (upper right).

The name conjures misty Norse sagas of Vinland, but no Vikings are known to have trod the shores of Grape Island. In 1775 colonists fought off a British party that was trying to harvest hay for the garrison in Boston. Since that clash, the island has remained undisturbed by military use.

Once largely agricultural, the island presents a peaceful, bucolic image. A house foundation and remnant plants are all that remain of a farming enterprise that lasted into the 1940s. Natural succession has created a woody and shrubby landscape on the former farmland, with many species of berries. Songbirds find this habitat appealing. In recognition of its agricultural heritage, the Friends of the Boston Harbor Islands and the Department of Environmental Management have installed a grape arbor near the pier.

Grape Island offers a good setting to contemplate the geological forces that have formed the harbor islands. The 54-acre island consists of two classic drumlins, one reaching a height of seventy feet. On the beach one can see glacial "erratics"—boulders dislodged from the surrounding till, freed to roll downhill or left stranded almost whimsically by the glaciers. Near the campsite entrance is an outcrop of the slaty rock known as argillite that forms the bedrock upon which later glacial deposits rest. This rock originated as slowly settling mud nearly 600 million years ago and on the other side of an ocean that preceded the Atlantic (not the ocean that exists now—see geology section later in this book). The marshy lowland between the two drumlins contains salt-resistant species such as Rosa-rugosa, cordgrass, and seaside goldenrod.

One of the rewards of island beachcombing is the discovery of a horseshoe crab shell.

Grape Island is one of a number of park islands that offers family visitors a chance to commune with nature in overnight campgrounds (photo, left). Visitors play cards under the grape arbor (photo, above).

Grape at a Glance

Access: Via regular passenger ferry service from Hingham or by the inter-island water shuttle.

Description: The island itself is actually made up of two drumlins—comprising 50 acres—that are connected by a marshy lowland. Wild grasses, sumac, and bayberry abound.

Facilities: A self-guided trail map is available. Composting toilets, picnic areas, hiking trails, benches are provided. There are seasonal rangers, tours, and special events. Individual and group camping is allowed, however, there is no running water or electricity.

Special Interest: Grape Island is known for its pastoral woods and trails, and features rocky shores and tidal flats, salt marsh area, and shell beaches. It is an excellent location for birding. Native Americans used it extensively for shellfishing.

Agency: Massachusetts Department of Environmental Management

GRAPE ISLAND
Existing Conditions

Island Accessible by Ferry or Water Shuttle

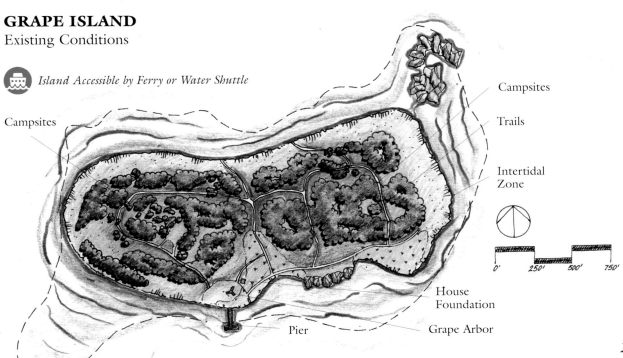

Campsites

Campsites

Trails

Intertidal Zone

House Foundation

Pier

Grape Arbor

Great Brewster

The outer group of harbor islands forms a distinct cluster often referred to as The Brewsters, although not all have Brewster in their name. They honor Elder Brewster, preacher to the early Plymouth colony. These islands are actually closer to the town of Hull, which once owned several of them, than to Boston.

Most of these islands are masses of exposed rock, sometimes covered with a thin skin of soil that supports sparse, windswept vegetation. Great Brewster is the one conspicuous exception, for it consists mainly of a towering drumlin. Despite erosion, it reaches a height of 105 feet, making it the highest point in the outer harbor and offering spectacular views.

After the retreat of the last glacier, perhaps 10,000 years ago, this high point would have been a prominent hill overlooking an undulating landscape—a tundra-like expanse, inhabited by subarctic plants and animals. Presumably other drumlins would have dotted this terrain, since it was sculpted in the same way by glaciers.

Now that landscape is only a geologic memory, recalled occasionally when fishermen's nets drag up the bones of extinct animals from Georges Bank. Great Brewster is the harbor islands' easternmost drumlin. The sea that has worn away and submerged neighboring drumlins still gnaws on Great Brewster. A 19th-century granite seawall protects part of the exposed shoreline, but erosion continues on the unprotected northwest side.

Great Brewster Island (photo, above) offers ample views of the adjacent Middle and Outer Brewster Islands shown on the horizon. Daisies are just some of the flowers that color the landscape on the islands (photo, below).

The island, which had been occupied by several farmers, was purchased by the city of Boston in 1848. This enabled the city to transfer it to the federal government, which proceeded to build the seawall. At the end of the 19th-century a colony of summer cottages was built on Great Brewster. Imagine the sense of freedom those people must have enjoyed on their breezy outpost!

Great Brewster represents the final phase of coastal defense, a story extending back to the early years of the republic. As weapons improved, harbor defenses became more dispersed and moved farther from the port they were protecting. In the case of Boston, Great Brewster was as far out as they could go. During World War II it was one of nine fortified islands in Boston Harbor and was the control center for the harbor's minefield. A battery of 90mm rapid-fire guns defended against torpedo boats. Foundations for crew quarters and

temporary buildings remain. They are a far cry from the massive walls of Fort Warren and reflect how our country's coastal defense system continued to evolve until the missile age made it irrelevant.

Great Brewster also figured in maritime safety. Bug Light, located on the long sandspit southwest of the island, warned of Harding's Ledge in the narrows off Point Allerton. Aptly named, the light was a squat structure perched

Groomed trails lead the Great Brewster Island visitor through thickets of staghorn sumac and other vegetation toward views of the harbor and its many other islands, including Little Brewster and Boston Light (at the horizon left in the photo).

Great Brewster at a Glance

Access: Inter-island water shuttle from Georges Island.

Description: At 22 acres, the largest of the outer harbor islands known collectively as the Brewsters. Comprised of two hills connected by a marsh and sandy beach, sand spits.

Facilities: Self-guided trail map available. Composting toilet, picnic areas, hiking trails, benches, seasonal park rangers, tours, special events. No running water or electricity.

Special Interest: Views of Boston Light and Little Brewster Island which lies just south of Great Brewster, World War II bunker, excellent birding, including cormorants and yellow warblers

Agency: Massachusetts Department of Environmental Management

on stilts and reminded people of an insect. The original manned light, built in 1856, was destroyed by fire in 1929. It survived long enough for its distinctive shape to become a popular subject on postcards. The light was rebuilt as an automatic facility in 1930.

At extremely low tide the southwestern sandspit extends nearly a mile, as if reaching for Georges Island. Other tidal flats extend toward Little Brewster and Outer Brewster Islands. For those with a sense of geological time, it is a faint reminder of the postglacial period when all these islands were part of a solid land mass. Today, visitors enjoy wild roses, tidal pools, and the drama of standing on the turbulent boundary of sea and land.

GREAT BREWSTER ISLAND
Existing Conditions

Island Accessible by Ferry or Water Shuttle

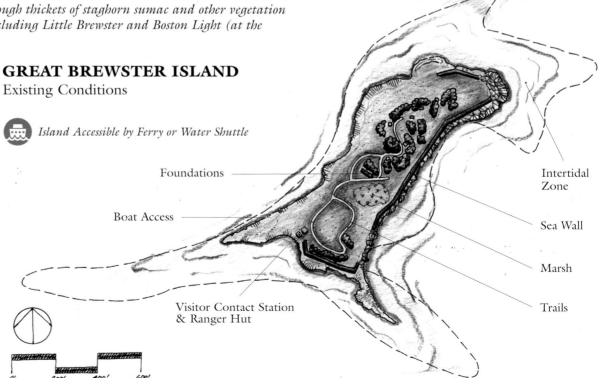

Foundations

Boat Access

Intertidal Zone

Sea Wall

Marsh

Trails

Visitor Contact Station & Ranger Hut

0'   200'   400'   600'

31

Hingham Harbor Islands

The cluster of tiny islands in Hingham Harbor—Button, Langlee, Ragged, and Sarah—could easily be called the Isles of Contrast, so much do they differ from expectations. Although surrounded by an urban area, they are surprisingly wild, with few traces of human habitation. They are relatively small in size—the islands together total only 15 acres—yet their vegetation and rugged terrain make them appear larger. Rock formations, dense undergrowth, and sometimes even aggressive gulls make accessibility to these

islands more challenging than their size and location would suggest.

Three of the islands (Langlee, Ragged, and Sarah) lie in the outer part of Hingham Harbor—not far from Worlds End—where it begins to merge into Hingham Bay. The smallest, Button Island, as round as its name implies, is located near the head of Hingham Harbor. All are predominantly outcrops of Roxbury puddingstone, partly covered by enough glacial till to support vegetation. The puddingstone is a tough conglomerate,

Sarah Island offers kayakers a backdrop where they can linger and plan the rest of the day.

different than the argillite that is the common bedrock beneath Boston Harbor, but approximately the same age.

Except for Button, these islands were purchased in 1686 by John Langlee, who ran a tavern and boatyard in Hingham. The three islands all immortalize in some way the name of Langlee's daughter, Sarah. As a child, undoubtedly enjoying the freedom of her island environment, she was nicknamed "Ragged Sarah." As an adult, she gained prominence by using her inheritance to found the Derby School in Hingham. Now Derby Academy, it is considered the oldest incorporated independent coeducational school in New England.

Once thickly wooded, the islands were cut over and, according to a late 19th-century description, had become barren and

Button Island is the smallest of the Hingham Harbor Islands and is located at the head of the harbor.

The rocks of Ragged Island display the plentiful cedar trees on the island.

unattractive. John R. Brewer, who then owned Worlds End, acquired Langlee and Sarah, and extended his replanting program on Worlds End to these islands. Wherever the native rock is covered by soil, dense vegetation flourishes. Langlee is noted for an enormous oak, while Sarah has a conspicuous linden tree. Ragged Island contains the remains of a small park or resort and, except for remnants of a pier on Langlee, is the only one of the islands that bears visible evidence of human activity.

Masses of exposed bedrock can be dramatic. Langlee Island, in particular, ends in an abrupt cliff on its northern side providing an unobstructed view of Hingham Bay. The Hingham Harbor Islands offer the same romance and diversity found on far-away islands without the need for an ocean cruise to reach them.

HINGHAM HARBOR ISLANDS
Existing Conditions

*Islands Accessible by Small Craft Only
(Protected Primarily for Resource Values)*

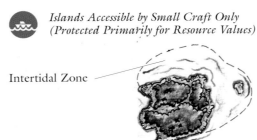

Intertidal Zone

LANGLEE ISLAND

Intertidal Zone

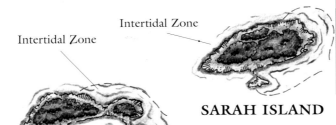

Intertidal Zone

Intertidal Zone

SARAH ISLAND

RAGGED ISLAND

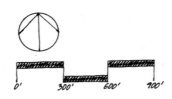

0'   300'   600'   900'

BUTTON ISLAND

Intertidal Zone

Little Brewster

Boston Light visitors get to explore the grounds where lighthouse staff live year round. A trip to the top of the lighthouse is one of the highlights of a scheduled tour.

Little Brewster is sometimes called Lighthouse Island, and it is easy to see why. Boston Light is its dominant feature, as is Fort Warren on Georges Island and the "eggs" on Deer Island. Only 3 acres in size, Little Brewster contains the lighthouse and its related structures, including the keeper's house, cistern, and oil house.

The present light, built of stone, brick, and granite, occupies the oldest lighthouse site in the country. The original lighthouse was built in 1716, more than thirty years before any other lighthouse in the present United States and at a time when there were few lighthouses in the world. The first lighthouse was financed by a tax of a penny a ton on all vessels entering and leaving the harbor. This structure was damaged by two patriot militia attacks and was then partially destroyed by the British when they evacuated Boston in 1776.

Rebuilt and relit in 1783, the tower was raised fourteen feet to its present height of eighty-nine feet in 1859. At 102 feet above sea level, the light is visible for up to twenty-seven miles out to sea under good conditions. In the other direction, from the top of the tower one can look across the majestic panorama of islands to the skyline of downtown Boston nearly ten miles away.

When the tower was enlarged in 1859, a second order Fresnel lens was installed. This lens contains 336 fragile prisms to magnify and focus the illumination and requires careful maintenance. The design specifications were lost during World War II, and thus the lens is irreplaceable.

By 1990 the Coast Guard had automated every lighthouse in the United States, with Boston Light scheduled to be last. Preservation groups appealed to Congress, and the decision was made to keep Little Brewster Island staffed. Coast Guard personnel remain, recording meteorological data in addition to maintaining the light and its related structures. It is a fitting tribute to the heroic efforts of the men and women of America's lifesaving service that Boston Light represents the last living link to the proud tradition of lighthouse keeping in the United States.

As a National Historic Landmark, Boston Light is recognized as one of the outstanding individual features of the Boston Harbor Islands. While the light serves to welcome ships to the portal of New England, its main purpose is to warn mariners of Shag Rocks, a treacherous outcrop just east of Little Brewster.

Boston Light is one of three lighthouses serving Boston Harbor. About three miles to the northeast, Graves Light, perched on another dangerous outcropping, performs a similar function. At 113 feet, Graves Light is the tallest. The third is Long Island Light, on Long Island Head, which marks the approach to the Inner Harbor. Other harbor lighthouses, such as Bug Light off Great Brewster and Deer Island Light, have been removed or replaced with beacons.

A one-of-a-kind Fresnel lens beams light in the tower of Boston Light out into Boston Harbor and the ocean beyond (photo, above). Boston Light (foreground) and Graves Light seem to stand side by side (photo, left).

LITTLE BREWSTER ISLAND
Existing Conditions

Island Accessible by Ferry or Water Shuttle

Keeper's House

Pier

Boat House

Oil House

Boston Light

Intertidal Zone

Cistern

0'   200'   400'   600'

Lovells Island

The mighty 10-inch guns, which were visible only when they fired, have long since been removed from Lovells Island. Their power is suggested by the thick concrete emplacements, which are likely to be around for a long time to come (in photo, bottom middle).

At first it seems strange to seek the romance of beachcombing in the middle of a great metropolitan area, but the wide, stony beaches of Lovells Island exert a timeless allure. From here it is the skyline of Boston that seems like a mirage, while the endlessly fascinating interplay of wave and shoreline is real.

The peaceful pursuit of beachcombing reflects the quiet charm of Lovells. As with many of the harbor islands, however, initial impressions are misleading. A hundred years ago this island, where children now frolic along the shore, bristled with guns. These fortifications were the product of what students of coastal defense refer to as the Endicott Period.

The Civil War had made it brutally clear that "Third System" forts, of which Fort Warren on Georges Island is a classic example, had become obsolete against improved ships and armament. The revelation that the system of "permanent" defenses had become useless almost at the hour of its completion staggered the military engineering establishment. Finally in 1885 President Cleveland directed his Secretary of War, William Endicott, to convene a board to develop a new approach to coastal defense. Following the report of the Endicott Board in 1886, a massive defensive program was carried out over the next twenty years.

The contrast between the Endicott System and the Third System is immense and unmistakable. Instead of looming vertical forts that concentrated tremendous firepower in one place, Endicott structures were dispersed and blended into the terrain so that they were almost invisible from the sea. Underwater mines, nets and other channel obstructions, torpedo boats, and elaborate fire-control and communications facilities rounded out the system.

Lovells Island was one of seven sites that defended Boston Harbor under this system in the early 20th-century. Fort Standish, named for the first military leader of the Plymouth Colony, is a representative example of Endicott work. It is supported by smaller batteries elsewhere around the island.

When the batteries were new, coast artillery officers sometimes introduced real or artificial plantings to conceal them. Nature has now assumed that function, and the once forbidding fortifications are gradually being cloaked and rendered less threatening by advancing vegetation.

Today's beachcombers spin their own fantasies. Most would probably be surprised to learn that if they had walked the same ground more than two hundred years ago they might have found grim reminders of maritime catastrophe. Probably the harbor's most famous shipwreck occurred in 1782, when the French warship Magnifique ran aground and sank off Lovells. Four years later a packet vessel wrecked, and all thirteen of the passengers perished on the island, including a couple stranded in the shelter of what is today known as "Lover's Rock."

Some good came out of that harrowing experience, as the incident led to the formation of the Massachusetts Humane Society. Beaches then were desolate and threatening places, where shipwreck victims often died of exposure. The Humane Society, which included many of Boston's leaders among its membership, erected "huts of refuge" on dangerous shores, equipped with a few necessities, to help stranded people survive until conditions improved. Boston, as the most advanced port in America, was a leader in this movement, as it had been in building lighthouses. One of Lovells claims to fame is that it was the site of the first hut of refuge in the United States (1787). None of these simple huts could possibly have survived two centuries of battering by storms, but the compelling story of the successor agency, the U.S. Lifesaving Service, can be traced at the Lifesaving Museum in Hull.

Swimmers and beachcombers find Lovells Island especially delightful.

LOVELLS ISLAND
Existing Conditions

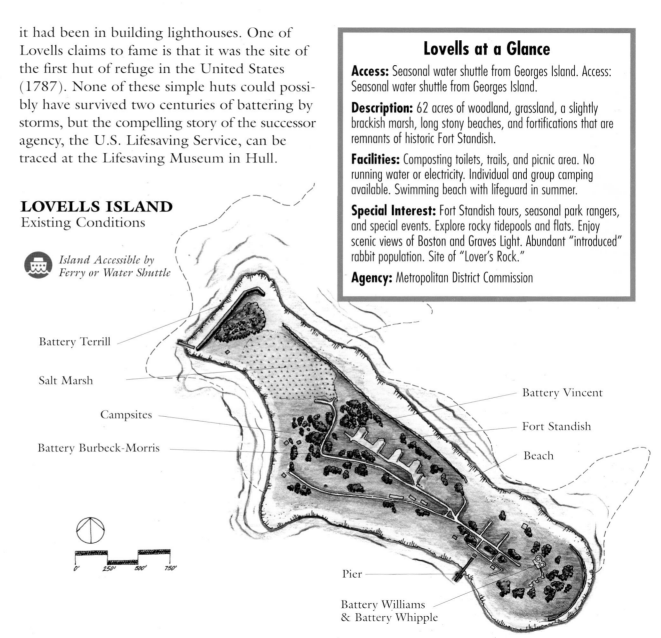

Island Accessible by Ferry or Water Shuttle

Battery Terrill

Salt Marsh

Campsites

Battery Burbeck-Morris

Battery Vincent

Fort Standish

Beach

Pier

Battery Williams & Battery Whipple

0'   250'   500'   750'

Peddocks Island

More like a cluster or an archipelago, Peddocks Island is comprised of five drumlins, the two largest of which lie side-by-side to form the eastern bulge of the island. The remaining three are connected by the low sandspits known as tombolos, with the smallest, Prince Head, having become part of the island only within historic times. Although Peddocks is the third largest of the harbor island group, it claims the longest shoreline.

The island looks like it wants to link up with neighboring drumlins on the Hull Peninsula, but the strong current in Hull Gut keeps them apart. Still, viewed from the island itself or from the surrounding waters, Peddocks looks like a series of separate drumlins rather than the single inksplash one sees on maps.

Until 1897 the military presence lay lightly on Peddocks Island. There was a brief encounter during the siege of Boston in 1775, when patriot raiders carried off livestock from a farm belonging to a loyalist. Later, patriot militiamen from nearby towns guarded the island against a possible return of the king's forces. Incidents like this, though seldom mentioned in history texts, were important in America's struggle for independence. By cutting off the British garrison in Boston from supplies of food and fuel, the rebels hastened the day when the redcoats were forced to evacuate the city.

Since the island did not face the main shipping channels, it was not fortified during the early phases of coastal defense. By the late 19th-century, with longer-range guns in the arsenals of both attackers and defenders, the strategic equation had changed and Peddocks' military value increased. At that time coastal defense was guided by the Endicott plan (described more fully under Lovells Island). Under the Endicott concept, a fort was no longer a single massive structure but a piece of real estate with gun positions and support facilities scattered throughout.

Beginning with a mortar battery in 1897, the U.S. Army expanded its presence until Peddocks became a major bastion of the Endicott era. By 1900, when the post was dedicated as Fort Andrews, it contained eight 12-inch mortars. (Mortars are artillery pieces that fire in a high arc so that the projectile descends on its target.)

A view of the East Head of Peddocks Island in the foreground contains two drumlins and shows the welcoming dock that leads to Fort Andrews. The three other drumlins in the background result in the longest shoreline of any of the harbor islands.

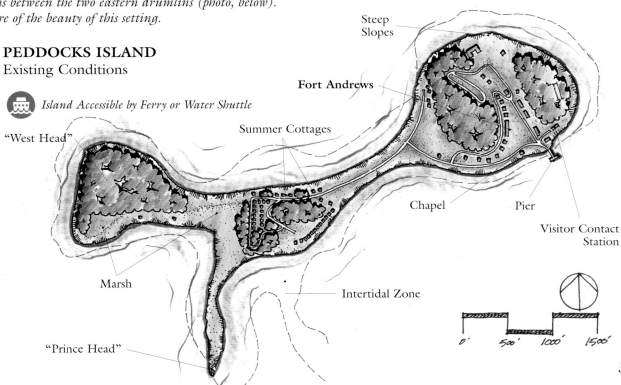

Peddocks at a Glance

Access: Seasonal water shuttle from Georges Island or passenger ferry from Hingham.

Description: More than 185 acres includes woodlands, fields, marshes, and rock/cobble beaches and sand spits. Peddocks is made up of five drumlins, one of which is connected at low tide by a spit of sand and gravel (tombolo).

Facilities: Composting toilets, visitors center, trails, picnic area. Individual and group camping available. Moorings.

Special Interest: Fort Andrews tours, seasonal park rangers, special events. Good sites for exploring and comparing diverse habitats—although you'll need walking time to get to them. Summer cottages on island.

Agency: Metropolitan District Commission

Kayakers approach the Chapel and camping area on Peddocks Island (photo, above). The tree-lined main street of Fort Andrews (straight, as one would expect) runs between the two eastern drumlins (photo, below). Military officers early in the 20th-century were fully aware of the beauty of this setting.

PEDDOCKS ISLAND
Existing Conditions

Island Accessible by Ferry or Water Shuttle

Steep Slopes

Fort Andrews

"West Head"

Summer Cottages

Chapel

Pier

Visitor Contact Station

Marsh

Intertidal Zone

"Prince Head"

0'   500'   1000'   1500'

Fort Andrews became more than just a gun platform. It was built into a full-scale base, with housing and all needed support for military personnel. Many of these buildings were constructed with redbrick walls and slate roofs, according to standard military plans. The installation resembles other coastal defense posts around the country, including some such as Fort Wadsworth on Staten Island, NY, that are managed by the National Park Service.

One group that was unexpectedly given a chance to enjoy the island's charm was more than one thousand Italian prisoners during World War II. These soldiers, who had probably been captured in the North African desert, must have thought they were being given a vacation at government expense. More than 1,000 American troops were also stationed on the island, making it a lively place.

The temporary barracks that housed the Italian POWs are gone now, dismantled by the army or by Hurricane Diane in 1954. Some twenty-eight of the older, permanent, structures remain. With little serious maintenance in fifty years, they are in various states of disrepair.

The island provides another example of the contrasting, seemingly incompatible uses that flourished on the islands. On Peddocks, although the army displaced one group of cottagers, colonies in other parts of the island coexisted with, and finally outlasted, the military presence. One group of cottages may have originated with a community of Portuguese fishermen. A majority of the harbor islands have been used at one time or another for recreation, but most resort structures, whether hotels or individual houses, have vanished. The remaining cottages on Peddocks Island are probably the best reminder of this activity, though they are gradually being removed.

A view over Peddocks Island shows how close it is to the City of Boston (photo, above left). This Metropolitan District Commission ranger is leading a tour through Fort Andrews (photos above). Previous page: Peddocks Island summer cottages are reminders of summertime recreation.

Rainsford Island

Rainsford is known for the graceful curve of its beaches with a view here that extends to Long Island Bridge on the horizon.

Surrounded by larger and more famous islands, Rainsford offers more modest charms. No gun emplacements bristle from its shores, nor did regiments drill endlessly, awaiting orders to distant wars. There were no lighthouses, rescue stations, or memorable shipwrecks to illuminate its tranquil history. Rainsford's past is largely agricultural and institutional.

Boston itself was in its first decade when Edward Rainsford, or Raynsford, acquired title to the island in 1636. He farmed the 22-acre island until his death in 1680. The whole agricultural period of the harbor islands, which lasted a century or more, is difficult to imagine. The trees that covered most of them when Europeans first arrived were cut over, converting the islands to a well-tended landscape of crops, orchards and pastures. Much of what we know about the islands'agricultural past comes from incidental reports early in the War for Independence, when British troops and colonial militia skirmished over provisions.

By then Rainsford had already passed from its agricultural to its institutional period. A quarantine hospital was transferred from Spectacle Island to Rainsford in 1737. As a busy port with ships arriving from faraway lands, Boston had soon felt the need for a quarantine facility. Rainsford Island, small and relatively secluded, but at the same time near the shipping channels and not too far from the city, was an ideal location. A 1780 map shows Rainsford labeled as Hospital Island.

The island's institutional heyday began in 1832, when the City of Boston erected a neoclassical smallpox hospital. Known as the "Greek Temple," it was the grandest building on any of the islands. Many victims of the disease were sent from Boston to pass their final months at the hospital and were buried nearby. Simultaneously, a summer resort flourished on the island's eastern head, a startling example of the seemingly incompatible uses that certain islands supported into modern times.

Much of the diversity of institutional use of the islands was represented on Rainsford. The Commonwealth of Massachusetts acquired the island for an almshouse in 1852. After the state abandoned the facility, it became a Boston city poorhouse. Still later, female paupers were housed here. Finally, the island supported the Suffolk School for Boys, a detention center. Their transfer around 1920 ended nearly two centuries of institutional activity on Rainsford, leaving a mysterious assortment of ruins.

Its gentle shape and relatively easy access for small boats made the nearly abandoned island attractive for outings. Many children were introduced to Rainsford Island through the generosity of George L. Randidge. One of those Boston philanthropists with very focused

The beach rose is one name for this prolific island resident that produces pink and white flowers and vitamin C-rich fruits called rose hips.

An inscription on Rainsford Island is testimony to its history as "Hospital Island," dated here six years before the City of Boston erected a smallpox hospital.

objectives, he created a fund that paid for island visits, so that children from congested city neighborhoods could spend a day on Rainsford. Hours of picnicking, games, and fresh sea breezes must have presented a startling contrast for children from crowded, noisy tenements, and it is no wonder that they and their descendants have continued to visit Rainsford Island. Birds also find it appealing, and it has become a favorite for birders.

RAINSFORD ISLAND
Existing Conditions

Island Accessible by Small Craft Only (Protected Primarily for Resource Values)

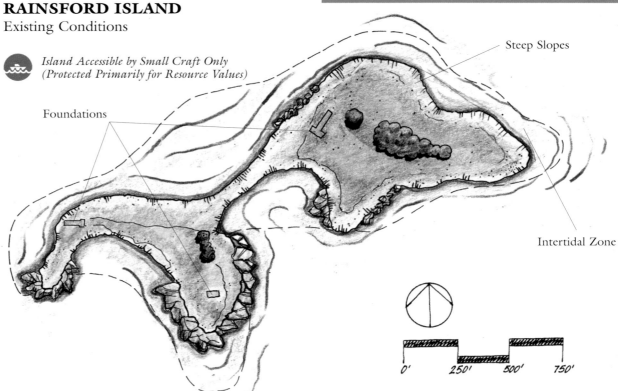

Steep Slopes

Foundations

Intertidal Zone

0'   250'   500'   750'

Spectacle Island

In the late 1990s, the city and state used fill from the underground highway project called the Big Dig to make Spectacle Island grow to its present height and configuration.

No island better symbolizes both the decline and rebirth of the Boston Harbor Islands than much-abused Spectacle Island. Once an appealing resort for Bostonians, it sunk to the status of a dump, infamous for its stench.

Spectacle's name recalls its charming early history. Initially the island was composed of two drumlins connected by a sandspit, which geologists call a tombolo. This configuration resembled a pair of old-fashioned eyeglasses.

In 1717 a quarantine hospital was located on the island, but this facility was moved to Rainsford Island twenty years later. By the mid-19th-century Spectacle's attractiveness and easy access made it a favorite resort for Bostonians. Two hotels were built, and illegal gambling reportedly flourished.

After this lively interlude Spectacle was turned over to uses that, while perhaps necessary, were less benign. In the late 1850s the island became the site of a factory that rendered dead horses for hides, horsehair, glue stock, bones, and neatsfoot oil. Essential to a horse-drawn society, this activity is one of the most malodorous known to man. Children of people who visited Spectacle Island for pleasure now held their noses as they cruised past toward other destinations.

Unfit for any activity involving human occupancy, Spectacle was used by the City of Boston as a solid waste dump beginning in 1921. This was the clearest illustration of treating the islands as an "edge" environment where activities that were unwelcome elsewhere could be carried on. Gradually the trash accumulated on the low portion of the island to a depth of seventy feet, giving it a saddle-shaped profile and altering the distinctive eyeglass form.

Garbage dumping ended in 1959, leaving the once-picturesque island a virtual wasteland. Underground fires that smoldered in the trash mound added Dante-esque commentary to three centuries of human stewardship. The abandoned and uninhabitable island became something of an embarrassment, and authorities were unsure what to do with it.

The prospect of renewal came from an unlikely source in the late 1990s. Fill excavated from the Central Artery/Third Harbor Tunnel project (Boston's "Big Dig"), was used to cap

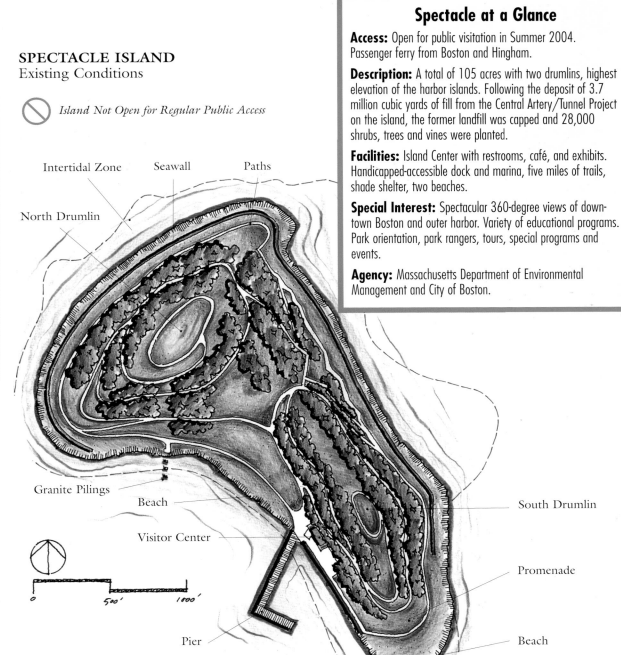

SPECTACLE ISLAND
Existing Conditions

🚫 *Island Not Open for Regular Public Access*

Intertidal Zone Seawall Paths

North Drumlin

Granite Pilings

Beach

Visitor Center

Pier

South Drumlin

Promenade

Beach

0   500'   1000'

Spectacle at a Glance

Access: Open for public visitation in Summer 2004. Passenger ferry from Boston and Hingham.

Description: A total of 105 acres with two drumlins, highest elevation of the harbor islands. Following the deposit of 3.7 million cubic yards of fill from the Central Artery/Tunnel Project on the island, the former landfill was capped and 28,000 shrubs, trees and vines were planted.

Facilities: Island Center with restrooms, café, and exhibits. Handicapped-accessible dock and marina, five miles of trails, shade shelter, two beaches.

Special Interest: Spectacular 360-degree views of downtown Boston and outer harbor. Variety of educational programs. Park orientation, park rangers, tours, special programs and events.

Agency: Massachusetts Department of Environmental Management and City of Boston.

Several years after Spectacle Island achieved its present height from fill brought over from the Big Dig, vegetation like the mullein shown here, common to other harbor islands, has taken hold.

the former landfill and create a landscaped park as one of the mitigation measures for the project

The island now commands the highest elevation in the harbor, offering spectacular views in all directions, and represents a magnificent symbol of renewal. All evidence of the island's checkered past has been obliterated and, with the Island Center, beaches, and paths, it will complete a tortuous return to its earlier uses, if not to its original form.

Thompson Island

Thompson Island provides a clear reminder of many generations of human attempts to manage social and environmental issues. The great age of social activism and experimentation began in the 19th-century. Out of this ferment arose the reform movements of abolitionism, temperance and women's rights, as well as prison reform, attempts to treat the insane, better sanitation, efforts to solve the problem of poverty, and so forth.

One of the favorite methods of the reformers was to isolate the dependent population. The harbor islands were ideally suited to this approach; after all, both "insulate" and "isolate" come from the Latin word insula, meaning island. From one point of view, this was another example of the islands as an edge environment, with society's unwanted being pushed to the city's geographic margins. This technique was in part self-serving, since it transferred disturbing sights from the crowded streets of Boston. Yet there was a positive side, for reformers believed that social problems were caused by the environment. Removing individuals from harmful surroundings was a necessary first step toward addressing their problem.

This is the background from which the first Thompson Island facility emerged. The Boston Asylum for Indigent Boys, founded in 1814, moved to the island in 1833. Two years later it merged with the Boston Farm School to form the Boston Farm and Trade School. According to the principles of 19th-century reform, the island's extensive working farm provided the

Thompson Island (photo above) supports open fields and wooded margins that allow island owners, Thompson Island Outward Bound Education Center, a wealth of choices to provide adventurous and challenging learning programs. To master the 60-foot tall climbing tower (photo, below) individuals must develop trust and promote team building, with the climbers depending on others on the ground to belay them safely.

setting in which destitute children "acquired habits of order, industry, and usefulness." The vocational farming emphasis lasted into the mid-20th-century, when it became apparent that it was futile to train boys for a declining occupation. A new academic curriculum coincided with a name change to Thompson Academy.

Today, owned and operated by Thompson Island Outward Bound Education Center, Thompson Island fulfills a vital educational role for children and adults from the Boston metropolitan area. The center is a non-profit organization whose primary purpose is to provide adventurous and challenging learning programs that inspire character development, community service, environmental responsibility, and academic achievement.

Although most of the buildings were built during the 20th-century, the complex represents a culmination of nearly two hundred years of effort in responding to social needs. In a larger sense, Thompson Island symbolizes Boston's use of its islands as a setting for dealing with the issues of an increasingly urban society. Massachusetts was traditionally in the forefront of social reform, and although particular theories may have been discarded or discredited, the Commonwealth deserves credit for grappling with these responsibilities at a time when turning a blind eye was the more common response.

Beyond the school grounds lies a rural landscape of fields, orchards, and winding roads that is startling but refreshing in a metropolitan area. Much of this is the legacy of the farm school, but the island was attractive to earlier inhabitants as well. Rich and close to the mainland, Thompson Island was frequented by Native Americans. It is the site of the earliest documented European use of the islands. French traders visited, and in 1619 (before Boston itself was settled) David Thompson built a post to trade with the Indians.

In addition to the ubiquitous drumlins, Thompson is representative of other examples of glacial craftsmanship. It contains a moraine, a formation created when a glacier halted and dumped its load of debris; and an esker, a sinuous formation which geologists believe was deposited by a stream flowing beneath or within a glacier.

THOMPSON ISLAND
Existing Conditions

 Island Accessible by Ferry or Water Shuttle

0'   250'   500'   750'

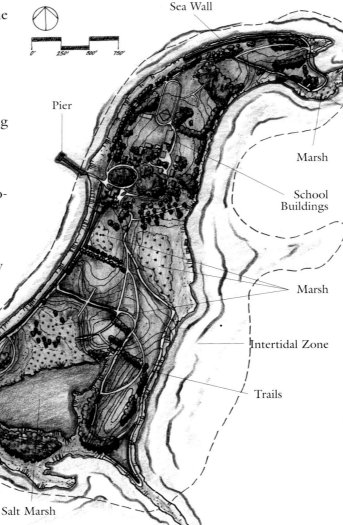

Sea Wall

Pier

Marsh

School Buildings

Marsh

Intertidal Zone

Trails

Salt Marsh

Thompson at a Glance

Access: Special ferry service. Open to the public on Saturdays between June and September; otherwise, visitors must schedule tours in advance.

Description: The island's 157 acres include a drumlin, moraine, and esker; open meadows; wooded areas; rocky and sandy beaches; tidal flats; a 50-acre salt marsh; and smaller marshes and ponds.

Facilities: Pier with floats. Restrooms, trails, and picnic areas. Buildings include administrative offices, conference and special event facilities, and a private middle school (The Willauer School). Year-round Outward Bound education facilities. No snack bar, but a picnic pavilion and two tents are used for functions. No private boat docking.

Special Interest: Self-guided trail map available. Salt marsh and beach habitat explorations, abundant bird life. Landscape and architectural features bear evidence of the former Boston Farm and Trades School, established in 1833.

Agency: Thompson Island Outward Bound Education Center

Outward Bound training includes learning how to sail and row in these 30-foot-long ketch-rigged pulling boats built in the 1800s for the Coast Guard. The boats are used on two-week expeditions when participants sleep on-board.

Worlds End

With the thickly packed community of Hull in the foreground, Worlds End is visible behind as a causeway-connected peninsula outlined by lush green forest. Worlds End is a superb example of how famed landscape architect Frederick Law Olmsted Sr. used his vision to define spaces and mark the land.

The great landscape architect Frederick Law Olmsted Sr. held aloft a vision for the harbor islands at a low ebb in their history. Decrying the "artificially bald, raw, bleak, prosaic, inhospitable" condition into which they had sunk, he proposed in 1886 a reforestation plan that would restore something of the appearance the islands presented when first glimpsed by Europeans some two hundred years before. In testimony to the low regard in which the islands were then held, the Boston park commissioners refused to appropriate the modest sum of $5,000 a year for six years to implement Olmsted's plan.

Shortly afterward, at Worlds End, Olmsted was handed a spectacular canvas on which to express his vision. Worlds End proper was an island consisting of two drumlins when first encountered by Europeans. These drumlins lay side-by-side, like those forming the east head of Peddocks Island. Colonists later enlarged natural deposits and built a causeway connecting the island to the nearest section of mainland.

This "mainland"—which in colonial times was occasionally an island during high tide—is composed of two more drumlins: Planters Hill and Pine Hill. Early agriculturists built two stone dams across the low area between Martin's Cove on the west and the Weir River on the east, creating the "Damde Meddowes" and tying the peninsula more firmly to Cushing's Neck, the nearest extension of the mainland.

Colonists farmed and grazed livestock on the fertile slopes of the hills. Even as adjacent Hingham Harbor and the Weir River developed shipping and other industries, the two pairs of hills remained bucolic, spared the institutions, fortifications, and industrialization that increasingly filled the shorelines of both the harbor islands and surrounding coast.

So matters stood in 1855, when John R. Brewer purchased his first parcel of land on Cushing's Neck. By the 1880s this wealthy but retiring Bostonian had expanded his estate to embrace nearly all of Cushing's Neck and Worlds End, and even two of the small islands (Langlee and Sarah) in Hingham Harbor.

The Brewer family raised agricultural use to a new level. At a time when traditional farming was declining in the region, the Brewer estate, though it might be classed as a "gentleman's farm," represented the first time the area had

The slender neck of sand and earth connecting the farthest drumlin on Worlds End to the rest of the peninsula offers views of Hingham Harbor islands and a place to play on the shore.

been combined in a single ownership and employed scientific ideas of management.

As early as 1859 the Brewers hired a gardener, who set out to "wage war on cedar trees" and began planting ornamental trees. (This was still on Cushing's Neck, as Brewer did not acquire Worlds End proper until 1864.) The Brewers kept purebred sheep; cattle, and numerous horses.

Olmsted's influence began sometime prior to 1890, when John R. Brewer asked him to prepare a road, landscaping, and subdivision plan for Worlds End and Planters Hill. Olmsted's curvilinear roads, still extant, follow the contours of the drumlins. Descendants of trees he planted, including many not native to New England, still thrive. Fortunately, the 163 proposed building lots were never developed. The planting program extended to the two Hingham Harbor islands Brewer had purchased in 1860.

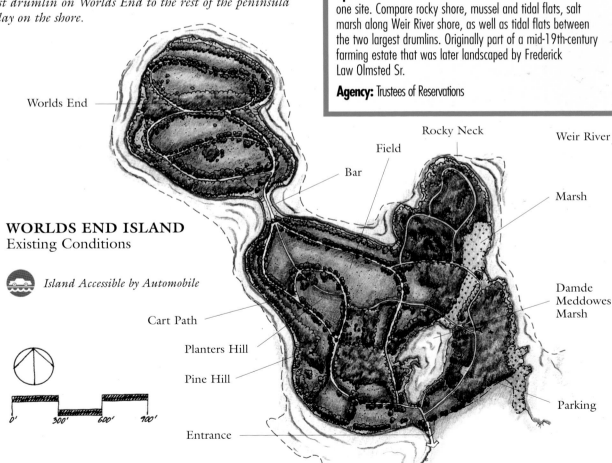

WORLDS END ISLAND
Existing Conditions

🚗 *Island Accessible by Automobile*

Worlds End

Bar

Rocky Neck

Field

Weir River

Marsh

Cart Path

Planters Hill

Pine Hill

Damde Meddowes Marsh

Parking

Entrance

0'   300'   600'   900'

An extensive array of bluebird nest boxes is sprinkled through many of Worlds End's grassy fields like the one shown here.

Old photos show horse-drawn wagons piled with towering mounds of hay grown on the four drumlins. As years passed, such bucolic images presented an increasingly sharp contrast to the densely built-up landscape of nearby Hingham and Hull. It is fortunate that when the last of John R. Brewer's children died in 1936 the Great Depression was at a low and development pressures were dormant.

In postwar years, however, residential building began to creep out onto the peninsula, and Worlds End was considered as a site for the United Nations headquarters and a nuclear power plant. Recognizing the threat to this exceptional landscape, in 1967, the Trustees of Reservations was able to raise funds to preserve Worlds End.

There is a historical fulfillment in this outcome, for Charles Eliot, founder of the Trustees, had been Olmsted's associate for a brief period in the 1890s. The two men, though far apart in age, shared similar conservation values. Eliot was probably the first to advance a plan that included the islands as valuable elements in a metropolitan park system. His concern for green space inspired him to found the Trustees for Public Reservations, ancestor of the present organization, to identify and set aside "surviving fragments of the primitive wilderness of New England...as the public library holds books and the art museum

The Damde Meddowes Marsh above is Worlds End's largest wetland area, made slightly brackish from tidal inflow through a broken dam. This strip of land (see map) was separated from the rest of Worlds End by salt water at high tide during pre-colonial time. 17th-century settlers built dams to reclaim the land from the sea. There are extensive strands of common reed (Phragmites) and swamp rose mallow here as well as plans for salt marsh restoration. Next page: Worlds End paths offer walkers and runners an ideal place for recreation.

pictures—for the use and enjoyment of the public." This was the first land trust in the United States.

The drumlins within the Worlds End reservation are probably the least modified in the Harbor Islands complex, retaining their original height and shape. Conversely, the Rocky Neck section exposes the raw bedrock that underlies the gentle drumlin formations, and the historic Damde Meddowes is now a brackish wetland.

Seen from the air or from nearby Hull and Hingham Bay, Worlds End has an almost unreal quality that quickly sets it apart. In a densely populated area it inexplicably contains roads lined with trees and open fields, but no houses. Seasonal changes in the colors of the fields and trees heighten its visibility but also the sense of isolation inherent in its name. Everyone who visits Worlds End comes away with the feeling that they have touched an exceptional place, accompanied by a sense of gratitude for those who have kept it so.

Island Geology

Boston Harbor is part of the Boston Basin, a lowland area beneath which there are sedimentary rock layers (consolidated layers of older, weathered rock, and/or organic or chemical matter) deposited at the end of the Precambrian time, about 600 million years ago. On the south coast of the harbor, these layers, called strata, appear in outcrops of Roxbury Conglomerate, containing boulders eroded by streams and glaciers from older volcanic highlands. Outcrops on the harbor islands themselves, including the Brewsters and Calf Island, belong to a shaly to slaty formation called the Cambridge Argillite (a kind of mud stone), which was deposited on the muddy floor of an ocean dating back some 570 million years. Argillite near Hingham contains fossil evidence of life forms pre-dating the "Cambrian explosion" of more familiar invertebrates, like the extinct marine organisms called trilobites, which were related to crabs and lobsters.

All of these sedimentary rock layers, as well as 610- to 590-million-year-old volcanic and granitic rocks surrounding the Boston Basin, originated on the far side of the ancestral Atlantic Ocean and drifted into their present position to "dock" with eastern North America. This we know from our understanding that earth's continents were once part of a super continent called Pangaea, which began to break apart through the process of "plate tectonics," and continental drift some 225 million years ago, and became the continents we recognize today.

In the past 100,000 years, during the Pleistocene Epoch of geologic time, two separate glacial advances formed hills called drumlins that cap bedrock formations of the Boston Basin. Boston itself is covered with drumlins —Beacon Hill, Bunker Hill, Winthrop Hill, Moss Hill, and Milton Hill—all smooth oval mounds of sand and gravel and larger stones left by moving glaciers, recognizable by their upside-down teaspoon shape. Rising sea levels following final glacial melting beginning approximately 16,000 years ago has "drowned" other drumlins to form the rounded summits of most islands in Boston Harbor.

Drumlins may occur as scattered single hills, or in so-called "swarms." The Boston Harbor Islands are a geological rarity, part

Seen from the shore of Calf Island (foreground of photo), Great Brewster Island offers one of the harbor's most dramatic examples of a drumlin, a hill of sand, pebble, and rock that was sculpted and formed by a retreating glacier.

Close-up views of Roxbury puddingstone, a conglomerate rock underlying much of Boston.

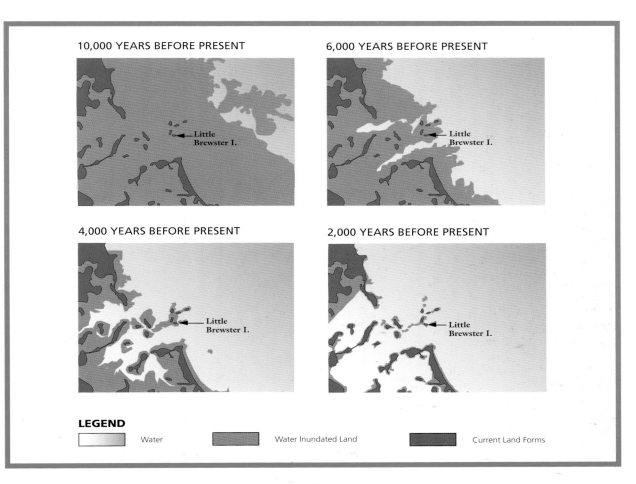

10,000 YEARS BEFORE PRESENT

← Little Brewster I.

6,000 YEARS BEFORE PRESENT

← Little Brewster I.

4,000 YEARS BEFORE PRESENT

← Little Brewster I.

2,000 YEARS BEFORE PRESENT

← Little Brewster I.

LEGEND

Water   Water Inundated Land   Current Land Forms

of the only U.S. drumlin swarm that intersects a coastline. This "drowned" cluster of about thirty drumlins are not all molded in the direction of glacial flow the way most other drumlins are. Geologists believe the islands are comprised of more than one drumlin and illustrate two separate periods of glacial action.

Like the glaciers, people, too, have continually modified the Boston coastline. When the early settlers arrived, most of Boston, South Boston, and Charlestown were peninsulas joined to the mainland by narrow necks of land. Often they would become islands at high tide. Eventually urban development led to the "filling" of several hundred acres of tidal flats, greatly altering Boston's shoreline. As a 1932 U.S. Geological Survey report noted, "Possibly nowhere else in the United States has the original extent and outline of a tidal harbor been so greatly modified artificially, chiefly through the filling of tidal flats."

Island Wildlife: Habitats, Fauna, and Flora

ROCKY SHORE, TIDEPOOLS, BEACHES, INTERTIDAL ZONES, MUD FLATS, AND SALT MARSHES

The rocky shores, tide pools, and mudflats of the Boston Harbor Islands are sources of endless fascination for the curious beachcomber and naturalist. They provide shelter and food-rich habitats for marine birds, mammals, fishes, and invertebrates, as well as nurseries for their young. Many of the wildlife species that inhabit the Gulf of Maine can be found in Boston Harbor, especially around the Brewsters.

Once-plentiful eelgrass is the only type of sea grass now present in Boston Harbor. Today fewer than 100 acres survive. Sea grass beds are critical wetland components of shallow coastal ecosystems, where they hold sediment, providing food and cover for a great variety of commercially and recreationally important animals and their prey.

Salt marshes, highly productive ecosystems dominated by saltwater cordgrass, provide habitat for many marine organisms. The largest remaining salt marshes in Boston Harbor are on Thompson, Worlds End, and Snake Islands. Smaller brackish marshes have been identified on Calf and Peddocks, while Grape, Slate, Sheep, and Raccoon have fringe marshes with cordgrass on gravel, shells, and cobble around the outside of the island. Mud flats, like salt marshes, occur in sheltered areas and can be found on Worlds End, Sara, Ragged, Grape, Slate, Raccoon, Snake, and Thompson Islands.

ANIMALS OF THE ROCKY SHORE, INTERTIDAL, SALT MARSHES, AND ADJACENT WATERS

Lobsters, crabs, clams, and seasonal white-moon and red lion's mane jellyfish live in the waters surrounding the islands. The zone between high and low tides (Boston Harbor's two daily cycles produce some of the largest tidal ranges in the United States, up to twelve feet) are home to familiar animals such as periwinkles, blue mussels, barnacles, limpets, slipper shells, and sea anemones. You can also

American lobsters find suitable habitat in waters of Boston Harbor (photo, above). Thompson Island's salt marsh sustains a rich community of life (photo, below)

find seaweed such as rockweed and other brown, red, and green algae there. Beaches reveal skate egg cases, horseshoe crab shells, the remains of sea urchins and complex mixtures of mussel, clam, and other ground-up shells.

Small fish such as mummichog and silversides, fiddler and green crabs, ribbed mussels, and mudsnails are just a few of the animals inhabiting the salt marsh.

Several other species of fish, including striped bass, bluefish, and winter flounder, live in or migrate through the waters surrounding the islands. There have been sightings of harbor seals hauling out on some of the outer islands. Because their feeding grounds or migratory routes are nearby, humpback, fin, minke, and North Atlantic right whales are potential, though rare, visitors. One can see white-sided and striped dolphins occasionally, and harbor porpoises visit the inner harbor in winter.

Sea anemones and sea stars live around the harbor islands (photo, top left and right). Sea birds seek rocky outcrops in the harbor away from busy boat traffic (photo, above).

Rabbits thrive on many of the harbor islands (photo, above). A clump of birch trees thrives on Grape Island (photo, right). Staghorn sumac and Pine trees are just some of the islands' more visible vegetation (photos, far right top to bottom). Staghorn sumac is the most populous of the sumac species on the islands, next to its cousin the smooth sumac. Staghorn can grow into tree-sized thickets, produce yellow flowers, and reddish maroon fruit like the one shown here.

ON LAND

A few species of land mammals, including exotic (non-native) species, occur throughout the islands. These include European hares, raccoons, skunks, gray squirrels, mice, muskrats, voles, and Norway rats. Some species have been known to devastate populations of small vertebrates and nesting birds. While no formal surveys have been conducted, the Eastern garter snake, Northern brown snake, and Eastern smooth green snake are known to occur on the islands.

TREES, SHRUBS, WILDFLOWERS

The harbor islands are part of an Eastern deciduous forest ecosystem extending to the ocean. They are a transition zone that contains species found to the north, evergreens such as hemlock and white pine, and species of pines to the south, from the coastal plain of Cape Cod.

Island vegetation reflects a long history of human impact and alteration, including the introduction of a large number of invasive exotic species. The islands' drumlins are thought to have been covered with mature forests of hemlock, maple, oak, pine, and hickory, which were cleared to support agriculture and pasturage, and to supply firewood for fuel. In addition, the construction of the islands' massive fortifications severely disrupted much of the native flora. Today the islands are slowly being reforested, a natural process called succession. Pioneer species including staghorn sumac, aspen, birch, white poplar, and pine are evident on most of the islands.

Some island vegetation was introduced by early English settlers or later by subsistence

The flowers of bittersweet nightshade are similar to related plants, the tomato and potato (above). Nightshade, however, produces a small green, then red fruit that is poisonous if eaten.

farmers. Pear and apple trees are examples of the species that have adapted well to their island environment. Grapes, asparagus, horseradish, chives, and garlic also grow wild on some islands, as do other edible plants such as beach pea, beach plum, and cutleaf blackberry. Introduced plant species include a kind of ragged fringed orchid, broad-leaved peppergrass, a twining vine called kudzu, the endangered seabeach dock, the tamarisk tree (national tree of Lebanon), and scarlet pimpernel.

Found on upper beach areas, scarlet pimpernel (photo above) grow low to the ground and spread out several feet wide. Flowers open and close depending on the weather.

Peppergrass (photo far left, top) has small oval fruits and is sometimes called poor man's pepper. It can form many branched clumps like the one shown here. The tamarisk tree (photo above, middle) on Gallops Island is also called a salt cedar tree because it tolerates living in a salty environment. In the spring it displays small pink flowers. It is not a true cedar tree and it is a relatively small tree in the harbor from eight to twelve feet. The beach rose (photo above, right) is common in many of the harbor islands especially around Hingham Harbor and the island group of Gallops, Lovells, and Georges.

Harbor Birds

The harbor islands provide good nesting and feeding opportunities for more than one hundred bird species including gulls, terns, herons, ducks, geese, hawks, plovers, sandpipers, doves, owls, woodpeckers, and perching birds. During migrations, large numbers of shorebirds flock to the mud flats and salt marshes around the harbor, while transient hawks and songbirds regularly make use of the more remote islands or those with suitable habitat. In late fall and winter, great flocks of waterfowl gather in harbor waters.

Summer visitors to the Boston Harbor Islands are as likely to see birds on the way to the islands as on the islands themselves. Great black-backed and herring gulls are some of the harbor's most familiar species, as are other water birds such as the common tern and the double-crested cormorant. Cormorants are visible on buoys, wharf pilings, and swimming at the surface, ready to plunge underwater in search of fish for their next meal.

Some birds use the islands as places to breed and raise their young. Most nesting occurs in the spring and summer months. One of the best places to observe summer nesting species is in the various abandoned military structures and buildings on the islands. Barn swallows are the most frequently sighted species. Fort Warren on Georges Island and similar forts and buildings on Lovells, Peddocks, and Bumpkin Islands are good observation points. It is best to view these nests, or any nest, from a distance.

Double-crested cormorants lay eggs on rocks and in nests in trees (photo above, left). Barn swallows nest inside harbor islands buildings (photo above, right). Oyster catchers stand out with their orange beaks (photo, above right, bottom).

For the off-season visitor to the Boston Harbor Islands, which are accessible through specially arranged tours, a host of different nesters and migrants awaits you. Dozens of species of birds—hawks, shorebirds, warblers, and songbirds—pass through this area on their way to spring breeding grounds or wintering areas. While you may see very few shorebirds in summer, you will find them in abundance during spring and fall. Other rarely seen species such as snowy owls may also be sighted at this time and in winter.

SUMMER SIGHTINGS

ON THE WAY
Double-crested cormorant, herring gull, laughing gull, great black-backed gull, common tern, ringed gull, Iceland gull, Bonaparte's gull

ON THE ISLANDS
Barn swallow, red-winged blackbird, yellow warbler, common yellowthroat, gray catbird, song sparrow, northern flicker, grackle

A great egret makes a careful landing near a nesting tree (photo, left). Blackcrowned night herons (photo, above) are usually well-hidden in tree thickets during the day.

ALONG THE SHORE
Double-crested cormorant, herring gull, laughing gull, great black-backed gull, common tern, American oyster catcher, killdeer, spotted sandpiper, snowy and great egret, black-crowned night heron, American black duck, ring-billed gull, least tern, purple sandpiper, dunlin

WINTER SIGHTINGS

BIRDS OF PREY
Snowy owl, short-eared owl, red-tailed hawk, northern harrier, northern shrike

SEA DUCKS
Common eider, harlequin duck, surf scoter, white-winged scoter, black scoter, long-tailed duck, bufflehead, common goldeneye, red-breasted merganser

GEESE
Canada goose, brant black

ALCIDS
Black guillemot, razorbill, thick-milled murre

OTHER
Yellow-rumped warbler, horned lark, snow bunting

Herring gulls lay eggs in a make-shift assemblage of straw on the ground (photo, above). Great black-backed gulls are aggressive foragers on harbor islands (photo, right).

Boston Harbor Bibliography

Bleiler, John. *A Field Guide to Thompson Island*. Boston, MA: Thompson Island Outward Bound Education Center, 1988.

Bunting, W. H. *Portrait of a Port: Boston, 1852–1914*. Cambridge, MA: Belknap Press, 1971.

Butler, Gerald. *Images of America: Military History of Boston's Harbor Islands*. Charleston, SC: Arcadia Publishing, 2000.

Commonwealth of Massachusetts. Department of Environmental Management. *Boston Harbor Islands State Park: 1986 Master Plan*. Boston, MA: 1986.

Dolin, Eric Jay. "*Boston Harbor's Murky Political Waters.*" Environment, 34 (6), 1992, pp.7–11, 26–33.

Dolin, Eric Jay. *Dirty Water Clean Water*. Boston, MA: MIT Sea Grant College Program, 1990.

Finnerty, Cheryl Anne. *Lighthouses of Boston Harbor Past and Present*. Seminole, FL: Harbor Productions, 2000.

German, Andrew W. *Down on T-Wharf*. Mystic, CT: Mystic Seaport Museum, Inc., 1982.

Jennings, Harold B. *Lighthouse Family*. Lower Cape Pub. Co., 1989.

Kales, Emily and David. *All About the Boston Harbor Islands*. Hingham, MA: Hewitt's Cove Publishing, 2001.

Kay, Jane Holtz. *Lost Boston*. Boston, MA: Houghton Mifflin Company, 1980.

Levering, Dale. *An Illustrated Flora of the Boston Harbor Islands*. Boston, MA: Northeastern University Press, 1978.

National Park Service, Boston Support Office. Boston. *Boston Harbor General Management Plan* (in press).

New England Aquarium. *The Boston Harbor Seaside Educator's Guide*. Boston, MA: New England Aquarium, 2000.

Perkins, William D. *Chestnuts, Galls, and Dandelion Wine*. Halifax, MA: The Plant Press, 1982.

Primack, Mark L. *The Greater Boston Park and Recreation Guide*. Chester, CT: Globe Pequot Press, 1983.

Sammarco, Anthony Mitchell. *Images of America: Boston's Harbor Islands*. Charleston, SC: Arcadia Publishing, 1998.

Snow, Edward Rowe. *The Islands of Boston Harbor*. Beverly, MA: Commonwealth Editions, Books of New England, 2002.

Snowman, Sally R., and James G. Thompson, *Boston Light: A Historical Perspective*. Plymouth, MA: Snowman Learning Center, 1999.

Sweetser, M. F. *King's Handbook of Boston Harbor*. Hingham, MA: Friends of Boston Harbor Islands, 2000, reprint.

Thomson, Betty Flanders. *The Changing Face of New England*. Boston, MA: Houghton Mifflin Company, 1977.

Walker, William H.C. and Willard Brewer Walker. *A History of Worlds End*. The Trustees of Reservations, 1973.

Whitehill, Walter Muir. *Boston: A Topographical History*. Cambridge, MA: Belknap Press, 1968.

The annual swim in Boston Harbor is sponsored by Save the Harbor, Save the Bay. The contest shown above began at a South Boston beach.

Boston Light occupies the oldest lighthouse site in the nation.